Animal Babies

Amphibians

Revised and Updated

Rod Theodorou

Heinemann Library
Chicago, Illinois

Customer Service 888-454-2279
Visit our website at www.heinemannraintree.com

Designed by Joanna Hinton-Malivoire
Printed and bound in China by South China Printing Co. Ltd.

11 10 09 08 07
10 9 8 7 6 5 4 3 2 1
10-digit ISBN 1-4034-9241-7 (hb)   10-digit ISBN 1-4034-9248-4 (pb)
13-digit ISBN 978-1-4034-9241-8 (hb)   13-digit ISBN 978-1-4034-9248-7 (pb)

The Library of Congress has cataloged the first edition of this book as follows:
Theodorou, Rod.
          Amphibians / Rod Theodorou.
              p.   cm. — (Animal babies)
          Includes bibliographical references (p.   ) and index.
          Summary: Introduces the birth, development, care, feeding, and
      characteristics of baby amphibians.
          ISBN 1-57572-950-4 (lib. bdg.)
          1. Amphibians—Infancy—Juvenile literature. 2. Parental behavior
      in animals—Juvenile literature. [1. Amphibians. 2. Animals-
      -Infancy. 3. Parental behavior in animals.] I. Title.
          II. Series: Animal babies (Des Plaines, Ill.)
          QL644.2.T469 1999
          597.8′139—dc21   99-17403
                                                          CIP

Acknowledgements
The publishers would like to thank the following for permission to reproduce photographs:
Ardea: Ken Lucas p. 30; BBC: Dietmar Hill p. 10; Bruce Coleman p. 12, Robert Maier p. 7, Jane Burton pp. **15, 25,** Phil Savoie p. **6;** Creatas p. **4** bottom left; Digital Stock p. **4** top right and middle left; Digital Vision p. **4** bottom right; FLPA: Chris Mattison p. 9, Tony Wharton p. 18, John Watkins p. 23; Michael and Patricia Fogden pp. **5, 13;** Getty Images / Photodisc p. **4** top left and middle right; NHPA: Jean-Louis Le Moigne p. 11, Joe Blossom p. 14, Karl Switak p. 22; OSF: Richard K La Val p. 17, Ian West p. 8, G I Bernard pp. 13, 16, 21, J A L Cooke, p. 24; Planet Earth: John & Gillian Lythgoe p. 14: Tony Stone: Robin Smith p. **20.**
Cover photograph of a frog with babies reproduced with permission of FLPA/Michael & Patricia Fogden/Minden Pictures.

Every effort has been made to contact copyright holders of any material reproduced in this book. Any omissions will be rectified in subsequent printings if notice is given to the publishers.

The paper used to print this book comes from sustainable resources.

Contents

Some words are shown in bold, **like this**. You can find out what they mean by looking in the Glossary.

Introduction

There are many different types of animals. All animals have babies. They care for their babies in different ways.

These are the six main animal groups.

Mammal

Bird

Amphibian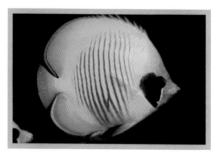

Fish

Reptile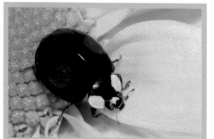

Insect

This book is about amphibians. Amphibians can live on land and in water. The babies often look very different from their parents.

As young frogs grow up, they look more like their parents.

What Is an Amphibian?

All adult amphibians:
- breathe air
- have soft, **moist** skin
- eat other animals.

moist skin

Glass frog

eggs

Most amphibians:

- live in fresh water, or near it on land
- lay eggs that their babies **hatch** from
- have four legs
- have a good **sense** of smell, even underwater.

This spotted salamander's skin stays moist, even if it is not in water.

Laying Eggs

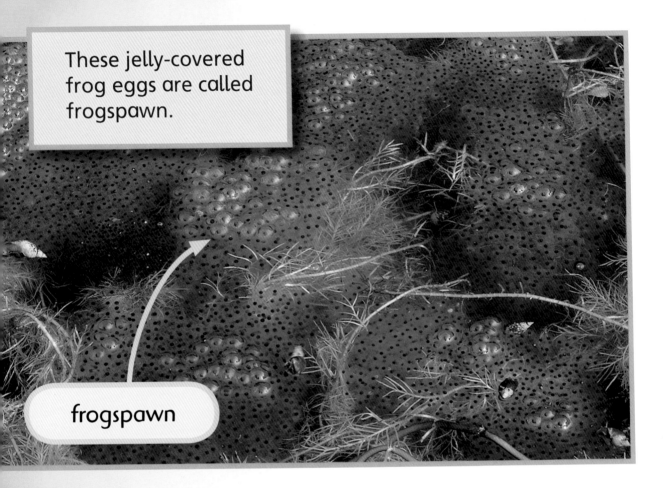

These jelly-covered frog eggs are called frogspawn.

frogspawn

Amphibians **mate** in or near water. Most females lay jelly-covered eggs in the water. The jelly protects the eggs. They grow very quickly.

The eggs are often eaten by other animals. The females lay many eggs so that some of the babies will live.

The female painted frog can lay up to 1,000 eggs at once.

Caring for the Eggs

The smooth newt uses its back legs to attach its eggs to water plants.

Some amphibians try to lay their eggs in places where other hungry animals will not find them. They lay their eggs under stones or attach them to plants.

Amphibians that live and **mate** on land cannot hide their eggs in water. They have to take special care of their eggs.

eggs

The male midwife toad carries the female's eggs around with him until they are ready to **hatch**.

Hatching Eggs

Some amphibian eggs are ready to **hatch** only a day after they have been laid. Others can take much longer to hatch.

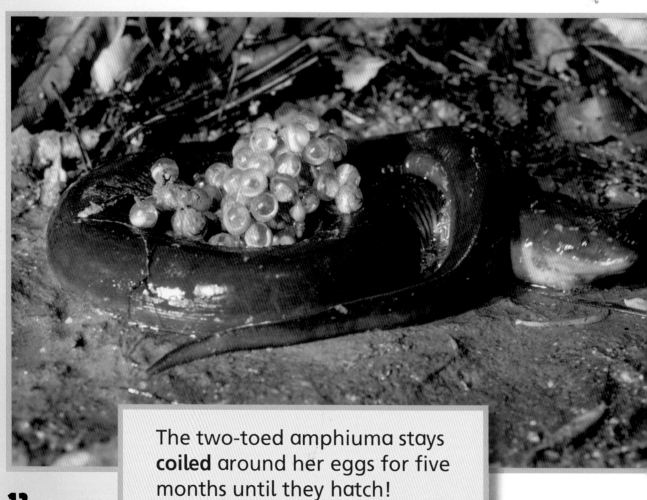

The two-toed amphiuma stays **coiled** around her eggs for five months until they hatch!

tadpole

egg

Frog and toad larvae are called tadpoles.

When the eggs hatch, **larvae** come out of them. Some amphibian larvae look like their parents, but most look very different. They have **gills** to help them breathe underwater.

Finding Food

Amphibian **larvae** are always hungry. They need to eat a lot of food to help them grow. Larvae that **hatch** from eggs eat the **yolk** from their egg first.

This tadpole is eating part of a plant.

tadpole

Soon the larvae have to find more food. Most larvae do not eat animals. They eat plants and **algae**. They suck them into their mouths.

Salamander larvae are unusual. They eat other animals, such as small insects.

Staying Safe

New **larvae** cannot move very fast. They are easy for **predators** to catch and eat. Water insects, fish, and other amphibians attack the larvae.

tadpole

This dragonfly **nymph** has caught a tadpole.

dragonfly nymph

eggs

This glass frog is guarding its eggs.

Some amphibians lay their eggs in tiny ponds or puddles where predators will not find their larvae. A few even stand guard over their eggs until they **hatch**.

Live babies

Alpine salamanders give birth on land to just one or two live babies.

Some amphibians do not lay eggs. They give birth to live babies. Their babies are born with legs. They are ready to swim and feed. Some are even born on land.

Amphibians that give birth to live babies usually live in places where it would be difficult to lay eggs.

This salamander lives in streams. If it laid eggs, they would be washed away by the water.

Amazing Changes

Amphibian **larvae** that live in water will change. As they get bigger, they grow legs. Their **gills** disappear. Soon they are ready to crawl out of the water and live on land.

These frog tadpoles have grown their back legs.

new back legs

The tail of this young frog has almost disappeared.

tail

Frog and toad tadpoles lose their tails as their bodies change. Newt and salamander larvae keep their tails. The skin may also become more colorful.

Living on Land

Many amphibians eat meat when they grow up. After they begin their life on land, they start to hunt other animals. They may eat worms, spiders, and small animals.

This huge African bullfrog will eat mice, other frogs, and even snakes!

Young frogs like wet weather. It is easier for them to move on wet ground.

Some amphibian babies stay near the ponds or streams where they were born. Others wander off and spend their lives on the land.

Unusual Amphibians

Some types of amphibians look very different from frogs, newts, or salamanders. They are shaped more like eels or worms. They live underwater or underground.

The caecilian lives like a worm. Some live underground and lay their eggs in a **burrow**.

This axolotl is an amphibian that looks like a larva all of its life.

Other types of amphibians look like large **larvae**. Their bodies never change. They spend all their lives in the water and never come on to land.

Amphibian Life Cycles

This is how a frog grows up. The **larva** does not look like its parents.

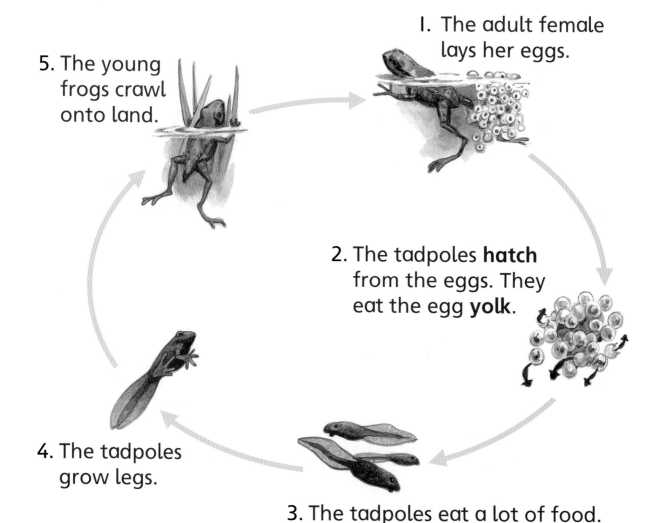

5. The young frogs crawl onto land.

1. The adult female lays her eggs.

2. The tadpoles **hatch** from the eggs. They eat the egg **yolk**.

4. The tadpoles grow legs.

3. The tadpoles eat a lot of food. They grow bigger and bigger.

This is how a newt larva grows up.
The larva looks a lot like its parents.

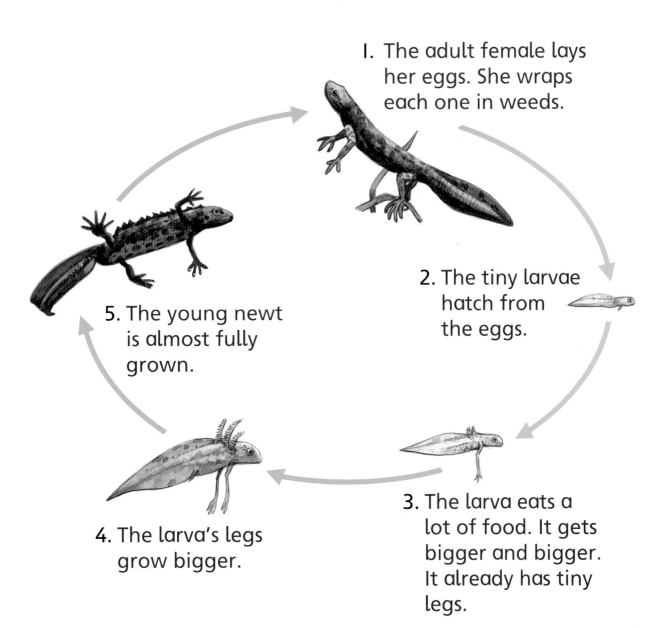

1. The adult female lays her eggs. She wraps each one in weeds.

2. The tiny larvae hatch from the eggs.

3. The larva eats a lot of food. It gets bigger and bigger. It already has tiny legs.

4. The larva's legs grow bigger.

5. The young newt is almost fully grown.

Amphibians and Other Animals

		AMPHIBIANS	
WHAT THEY LOOK LIKE:	Bones inside body	all	
	Number of legs	4 or none	
	Hair on body	none	
	Scaly skin	none	
	Wings	none	
	Feathers	none	
WHERE THEY LIVE:	On land	most	
	In water	some	
HOW THEY ARE BORN:	Grows babies inside body	few	
	Lays eggs	most	
HOW THEY FEED BABIES:	Feeds baby milk	none	
	Brings baby food	none	

  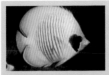  

MAMMALS	INSECTS	FISH	BIRDS	REPTILES
all	none	all	all	all
none, 2, or 4	6	none	2	4 or none
all	all	none	none	none
few	none	most	none	all
some	most	none	all	none
none	none	none	all	none
most	most	none	all	most
some	some	all	none	some
most	some	some	none	some
few	most	most	all	most
all	none	none	none	none
most	some	none	most	none

Amazing Amphibians

- The smallest frog is the gold frog. When it is fully grown, it is only about the size of your fingernail.

- When the first frog appeared on Earth, dinosaurs were still alive.

- The biggest amphibian is the Japanese giant salamander. It can be as long as an adut lying down!

Giant salamander

Glossary

algae (one is an alga) very small plants that grow in water or damp places

burrow hole that an animal makes in the ground to live or hide eggs in

coiled to be wrapped around in a circle

gill part of an amphibian or fish's body that takes oxygen from water to help it breathe

hatch to be born from an egg

larva (more than one are larvae) animal baby that hatches from an egg but looks different from an adult

mate when a male and a female animal make babies

moist little wet

nymph young insect that looks very like an adult insect when it is born

predator animal that hunts and kills other animals for food

sense to be able to feel, see, smell, hear, or taste something

yolk part of an egg that is food for a baby animal

Find out More

Books

Ganeri, Anita. *From Tadpole to Frog*. Chicago: Heinemann Library, 2006.

Miles, Elizabeth. *Watching Tree Frogs in South America*. Chicago: Heinemann Library, 2006.

Websites

www.allaboutfrogs.org

www.nationalgeographic.com/kids/creature_feature/0203/frogs.html

Index